.com * C++

HOW DO COMPUTERS FOLLOW INSTRUCTIONS?

A BOOK ABOUT PROGRAMMING

JAVA

C++

C

Python

written by j.t. liso
illustrated by srimalie bassani

W9-BWD-062

How do computers follow instructions so well? Do they have giant ears so they can listen closely? Computers always do exactly what they are told to do and they do it quickly because they are designed to run on instructions. We call those instructions computer programs.

We write computer programs to instruct a computer on what it is we need it to do. Programs are a set of directions. They may seem complicated, but programs are actually quite simple. It is important to get the program right because the computer is going to do what the program tells it to do—even if you accidentally tell it to do the wrong thing!

How do we communicate with computers?
Do we have to hire a translator to translate the instructions
from English to a secret computer language?

Translator?!?! No way! Well, sort of...

Programs are written in different programming languages. Even though programs are all very different in the way they are written, a computer can understand all of them! This is because each language has a feature known as a compiler that changes the programming language into instructions the computer can understand. So the compiler is sort of like a translator.

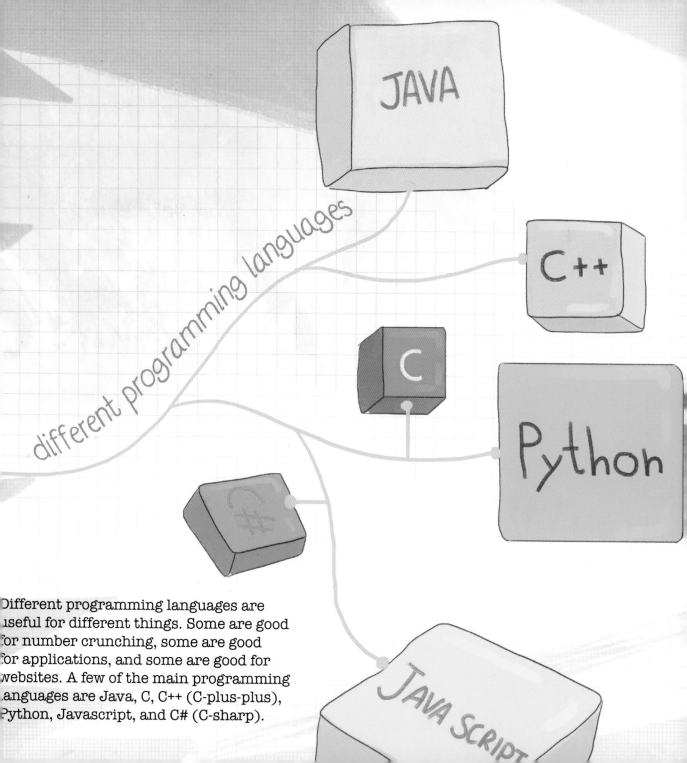

different programming languages

Different programming languages are useful for different things. Some are good for number crunching, some are good for applications, and some are good for websites. A few of the main programming languages are Java, C, C++ (C-plus-plus), Python, Javascript, and C# (C-sharp).

How do programs communicate between computers and users?
Do they use cell phones to call or text us when it is time to run the program?

A cell phone?!?! No way!

Computers, programs, and users interact through inputs and outputs.

1 Users can give the input using the mouse or keyboard.

2 The computer can give the output to the user through the monitor, speakers, or printer.

INPUT

MONITOR

OUTPUT

PRINTER/SCANNER

It is very important for computers and users to talk to each other. The input is the information the user provides and the output is what the computer returns. Inputs and outputs come in many different forms, and they change based on what the program is doing. Sometimes the input of a program is a file and the output is the message to the computer screen. Sometimes the input is the button you press and the output is what happens on the screen. When the input we give gets the output we want, we know the program is working.

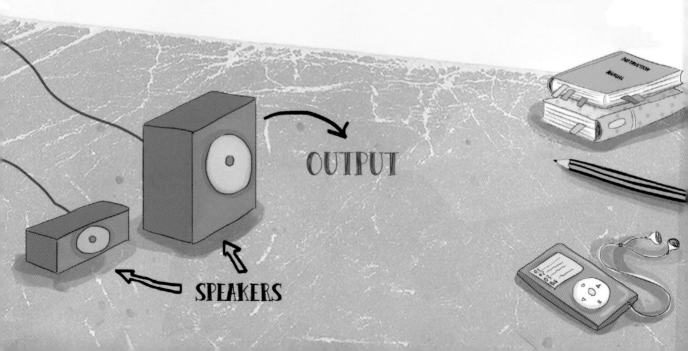

OUTPUT

SPEAKERS

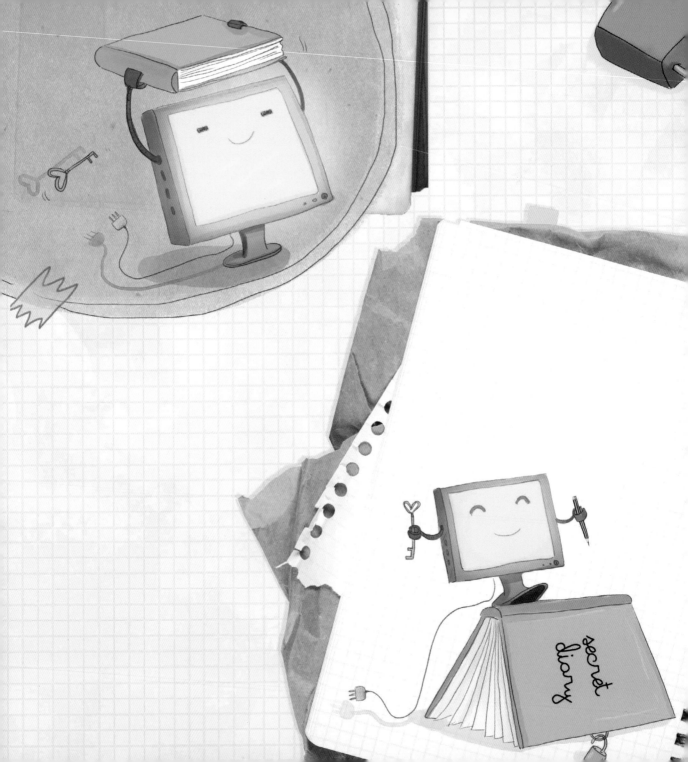

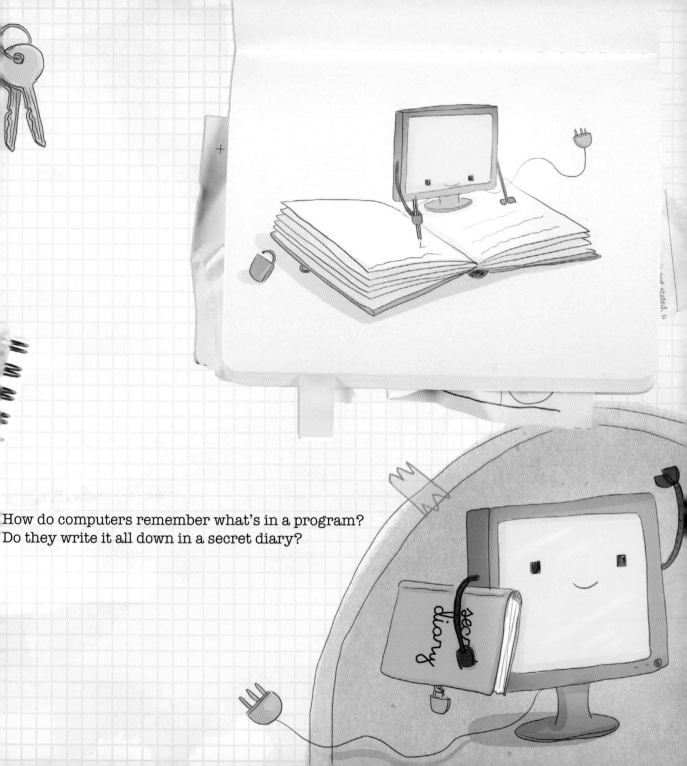

How do computers remember what's in a program?
Do they write it all down in a secret diary?

Secret diary?!?! No way!

The information stored in a program is called data, and data is stored in variables. Variables are a way to name a specific storage location in a program so the program can remember it easily. There are many different types of variables.

For example, there are whole numbers known as INTEGERS which are positive or negative numbers that do not include fractions or decimals.

-10 -9 -8 -7 -6 -5 -4 -3 -2 -1 0 1 2 3 4 5 6 7 8 9 10

integers

Is 7 an integer?

Yes.

Is 7.5 an integer?

No.

Is -1,000,000 an integer?

Yes.

Is 7,234,643,932 a...

STOP! This could go on forever!

There are also variables called FLOATS which are fractional numbers with a decimal point.

And finally, there are BOOLEANS which are variables that are stored with only one of two choices—true or false.

How do computers do math so quickly?
Do they have a giant calculator handy to help them solve math problems?

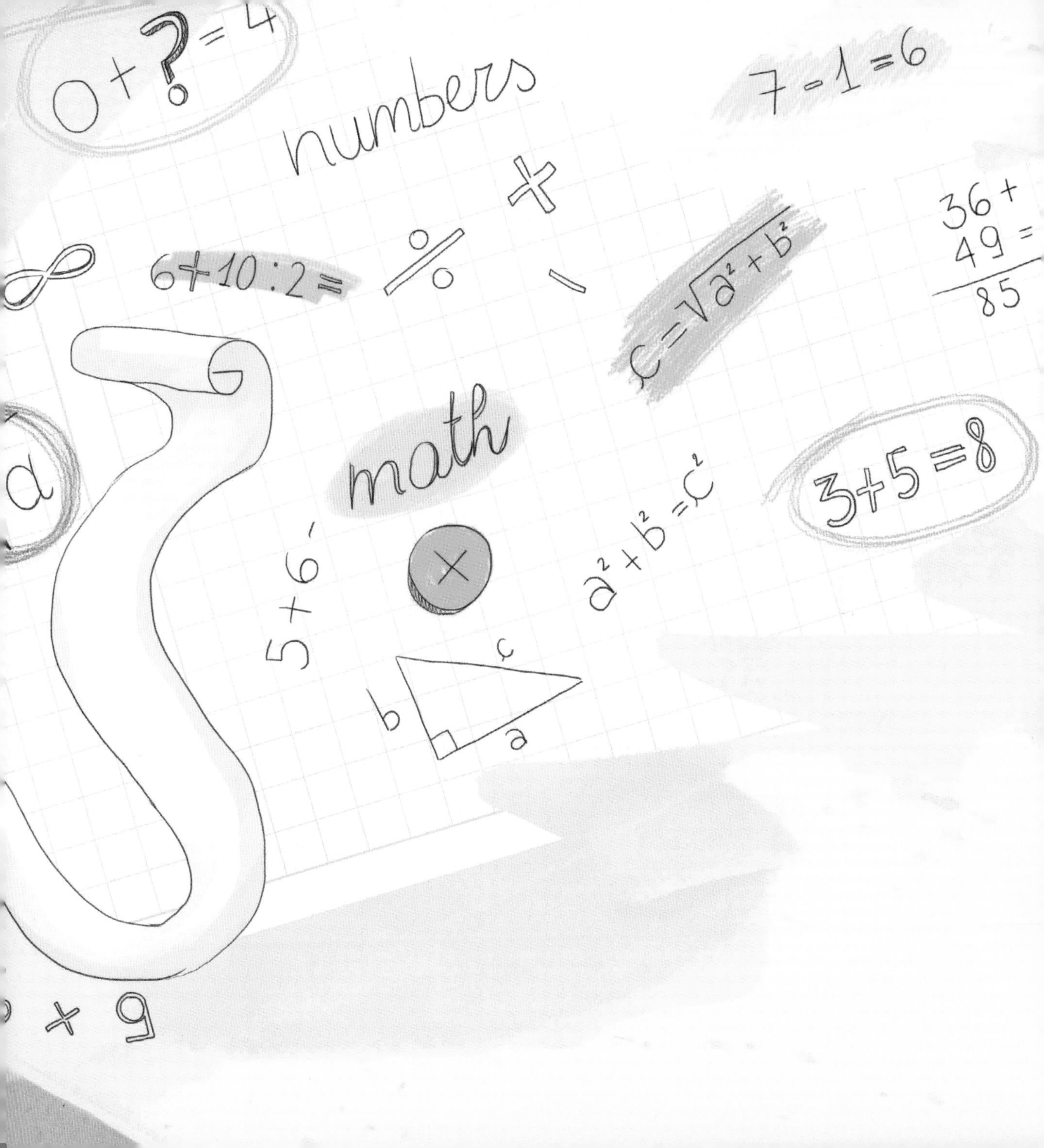

$0 + ? = 4$

numbers

$7 - 1 = 6$

∞

$6 + 10 : 2 =$

$\div$

$+$

$-$

$c = \sqrt{a^2 + b^2}$

$\begin{array}{r} 36 + \\ 49 = \\ \hline 85 \end{array}$

a

math

$5 + 6 -$

$\times$

$a^2 + b^2 = c^2$

$3 + 5 = 8$

c

b

a

$6 + 9$

A calculator?!?! No way!

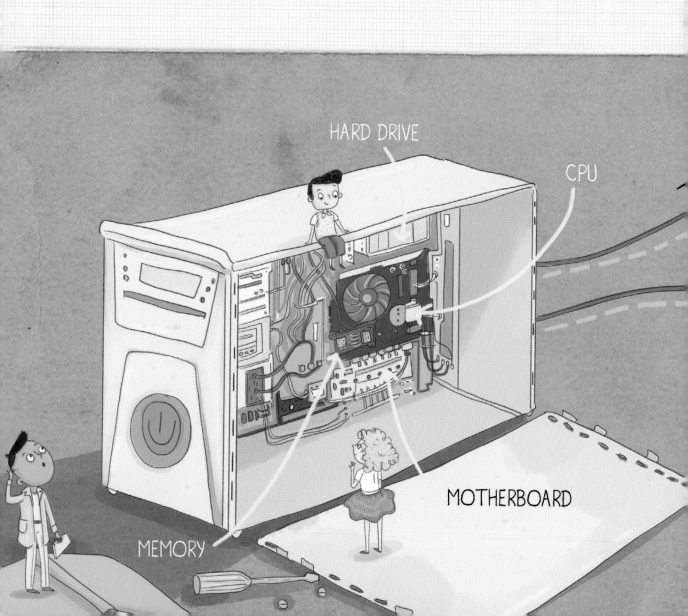

binary code

omputers don't need calculators, because they can calculate math all on their own!

computer has all of the tools to solve math equations programmed into it.
he computer changes all of the data it receives into binary code. Binary code is the
omputer's language. Binary code consists of character strings of only zeros and ones.
he computer uses a chip called the CPU (central processing unit) to solve the problem in
inary code. Then the result is stored in a variable that the program can use. So really, the
omputer is a high-powered calculator all on its own!

How do computers know how to decide which tasks to complete?
Do they just flip a coin?

Flip a coin?!?! No way!

Computers use logic statements. We write logic statements into our computer's program to tell the computer which tasks to complete.

Remember Booleans, the variables that represent true or false? These variables serve as the basis for computer logic. We can use Booleans for many different things. We can determine if a number is greater than, equal to, or less than another number using Booleans.

Is 6 greater than 7?

False!

Is 6 equal to 7?

False!

Is 6 less than 7?

True!

true

false

Booleans can also be used to make "if-else" statements. If-else statements are used to move the computer's processing in a new direction based on whether the Boolean value is true or false. This allows computers to solve more complicated problems, because they can consider different answers and then move forward based on the results.

IF something is true...

Do this.

ELSE...

Do that.

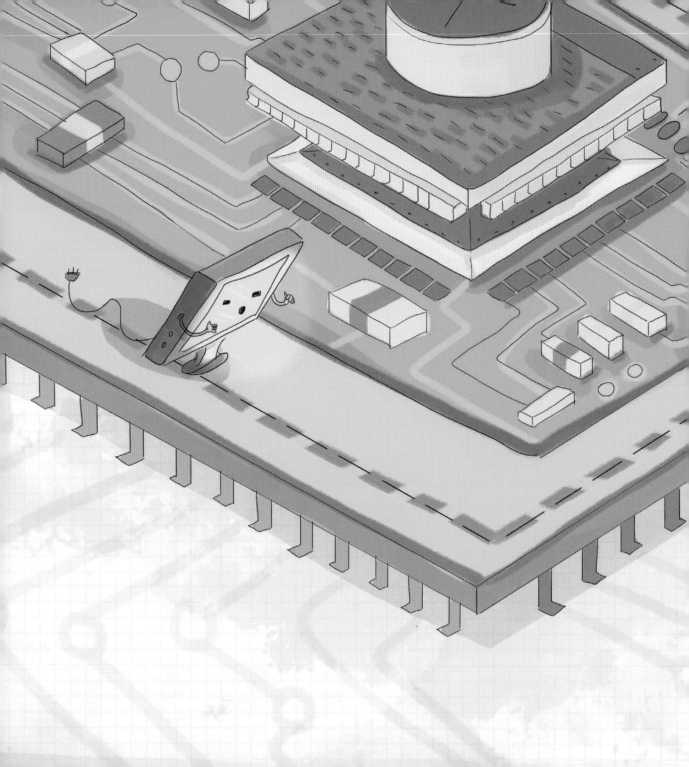

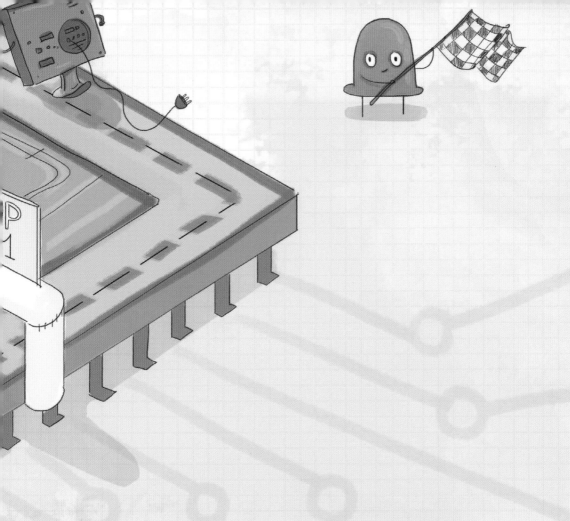

How do computers know to repeat a task over and over again?
Do they just run around a track until they are tired and then quit?

A track?!?! No way!

Computers use loops to repeat a given task. There are two different types of loops that we can program. The two types of loops are called "for" loops and "while" loops. "For" loops walk through a series of tasks by designating a place to start and a place to end. "While" loops have a Boolean that keeps checking back in. They repeat the loop while the Boolean is true and stop when the Boolean changes to false.

PROGRAMS ALL AROUND US

We can see examples of programming every single day. A lot of technology we use is programmed to function the way we want and expect it to. Here are a few examples:

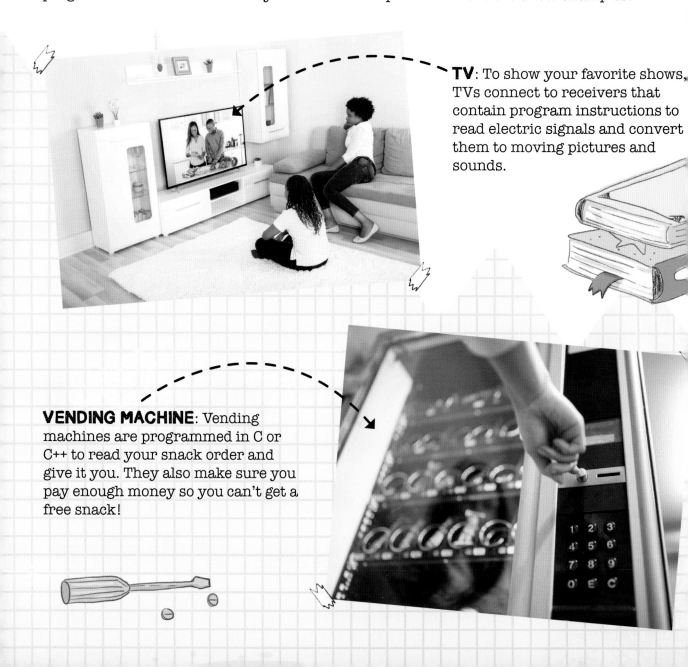

TV: To show your favorite shows, TVs connect to receivers that contain program instructions to read electric signals and convert them to moving pictures and sounds.

VENDING MACHINE: Vending machines are programmed in C or C++ to read your snack order and give it you. They also make sure you pay enough money so you can't get a free snack!

MICROWAVE: Microwaves are programmed with timers so that your food can cook for the proper amount of time.

FITNESS TRACKER: Fitness trackers use program instructions to detect how quickly you are moving in order to count your steps and average speed!

CELL PHONE: Cell phones are actually programmed a lot like computers. They have a main circuit board and operating system that handles all of the processing and tasks.

WIRELESS HEADPHONES: Wireless headphones are programmed to pick up Bluetooth signals that contain sound. They function a lot like miniature radios using short-range Bluetooth signals instead of long-range radio waves.

LAPTOP: Laptops contain a central processing unit (CPU) that uses program instructions to decide how to process different instructions from applications.

AMING CONSOLE: Gaming
onsoles are like computers.
hey contain software called
ngines that are similar to
perating systems for each
ame. These engines are
rogrammed to display the
ame graphics and handle all of
ne action for a fun experience!

GLOSSARY

Application – a program or type of software created to complete a task for the user

Binary Code – a programming system that uses zeros and ones to represent letters, digits, and other characters

Boolean – a type of variable with two possible values: true or false

Central Processing Unit – the part of a computer where operations are controlled and executed

Character – any letter, number, symbol, or even a space that you can type on your computer

Character String – a sequence of characters organized into a variable

Compiler – a program that converts instructions into something the computer can understand

Computer Program – a list of instructions required for a computer to complete a task

Data – information that is processed and stored by the computer

Float – a type of variable with a fractional value, meaning it is a number with a decimal point

For Loop – a sequence of instructions that repeats a specified number of times

Hard Drive – the place where data is stored within a computer

If-Else Statement – instructions given to a program to complete a given task while the condition is true but then change the task when the same condition becomes false

Input – any information or data that is sent to a computer through an input device

Instructions – a sequence in a computer program that defines an operation or task

Integer – a type of variable that is a whole number that can be either negative, positive, or zero

Logic Statements – programming instructions provided by the user

Loop – a sequence of instructions in a program that is continually repeated until a certain condition is reached

Memory – the part of a computer where data and instructions can be stored and used

Motherboard – the home of many of the important components of a computer

Output – data produced by the computer and delivered through an output device

Processing – a program operating on input to produce an output

Programming Language – a set of commands or instructions used to create a program

Task – a basic unit of computer programming that describes a desired output from a selected input

User – a person who is operating a computer and providing inputs

Variable – data that can change depending on the conditions or information in a program

While Loop – a sequence of instructions that continues as long as a specified condition is true and ends when the condition changes